A FIRST POETRY BOOK

compiled by John Foster

illustrated by
Chris Orr
Martin White
Joseph Wright

Oxford University Press 1979

Oxford University Press, Walton Street, Oxford OX2 6DP

Oxford   London   Glasgow
New York   Toronto   Melbourne   Wellington
Ibadan   Nairobi   Dar es Salaam   Cape Town
Kuala Lumpur   Singapore   Jakarta   Hong Kong   Tokyo
Delhi   Bombay   Calcutta   Madras   Karachi

Typeset by Tradespools Ltd, Frome
Printed by Chorley and Pickersgill Ltd, Leeds

Contents

Can't Wait	John Kitching	7
This is the hand	Michael Rosen	8
Hands	Peter Young	9
The Broken Toys	James Kirkup	10
Balloons!	Judith Thurman	11
Father says	Michael Rosen	12
What someone said when he was spanked on the day before his birthday	John Ciardi	13
Hurry Home	Leonard Clark	14
Sad . . . and Glad	Brian Lee	15
Flashlight	Judith Thurman	16
It's dark outside	Nancy Chambers	17
The sounds in the evening	Eleanor Farjeon	18
The Park	James S. Tippett	20
In The Dark	Jane Pridmore	21
The Bogus-Boo	James Reeves	22
I woke up this morning	Karla Kuskin	24
The Quarrel	Eleanor Farjeon	26
She said I said he lied	Michael Rosen	27
I'm the youngest in our house	Michael Rosen	28
My sister Laura	Spike Milligan	29
Going Through the Old Photos	Michael Rosen	30
When we go over to my grandad's	Michael Rosen	31
Zanzibar Pete and Zoom-along Dick	Nancy Chambers	32
The Vulture	Hilaire Belloc	33
Toffee-Slab	Brian Lee	34
Sweet Song	Vernon Scannell	35
When Dad felt bad	Charles Causley	36
The Dustbin Men	Gregory Harrison	38
Mud	John Smith	40
Building Site	Marian Lines	41
Motor Cars	Rowena Bastin Bennett	42
The Old Sussex Road	Ian Serraillier	42

Carbreakers	Marian Lines	43
Let's send a rocket	Kit Patrickson	44
The Aeroplane	Derek Stuart	45
The cliff-top	Robert Bridges	46
The Ship	Richard Church	47
Going Barefoot	Judith Thurman	48
Sea Shore	John Kitching	49
Seal	William Jay Smith	50
Flute Girl	Roderick Hunt	51
The Rescue	Ian Serraillier	52
Bones	Brian Lee	54
Greedy Dog	James Hurley	55
Roger the Dog	Ted Hughes	56
Cats	Eleanor Farjeon	58
Cat	Vernon Scannell	59
Yellow Cat	Gregory Harrison	60
Grumblers	Leonard Clark	62
Mare	Judith Thurman	63
The small brown bear	Michael Baldwin	64
Arctic Vixen	Michael Baldwin	65
Gabble-Gabble	James Reeves	66
Porwigles	Julie Holder	68
The Frog's Lament	Aileen Fisher	70
A centipede	Julie Holder	72
Slugs	John Kitching	73
A Dragonfly	Eleanor Farjeon	74
August afternoon	Marion Edey	75
There's a red brick wall	Nancy Chambers	76
Swimming in the town	Ian Serraillier	77
The Pines	Margaret Mahy	78
Holes of green	Aileen Fisher	79
What is Red	Mary O'Neill	80
The Kite	Harry Behn	82

The Wind	James Reeves	84
Clouds	Aileen Fisher	85
Windy Nights	Robert Louis Stevenson	86
Flying	J. M. Westrup	87
The night will never stay	Eleanor Farjeon	88
Winter Morning	Ogden Nash	90
Death of a snowman	Vernon Scannell	91
There was an old man	James Kirkup	92
Giant Jojo	Michael Rosen	93
Alone in the Grange	Gregory Harrison	94
Uncle James	Margaret Mahy	96
Dan the watchman	John D. Sheridan	98
Herbaceous Plodd	Michael Dugan	100
Rosemary's teeth	Michael Dugan	101
Scarecrow Independence	James Kirkup	102
Ella McStumping	Michael Dugan	103
Thin Jake	Michael Dugan	104
The radio men	Elizabeth Jennings	105
The Little Wee Man	Ian Serraillier	106
The Marrog	R. C. Scriven	108
Mixed Brews	Clive Sansom	110
House	Leonard Clark	112
The Man Who Wasn't There	Brian Lee	113
The Silent Spinney	Seamus Redmond	114
Hide and Seek	Robert Graves	115
Cold Feet	Brian Lee	116
Lonely boy	John Kitching	117
What?	Brian Lee	118
Closet	Judith Thurman	119
Secrets	Edward Lowbury	120
The Spinning Earth	Aileen Fisher	121
I wonder	Jeannie Kirby	122
Who?	Jane Catermull	123

Can't Wait

Not having much fun
At One.

In a cage (like a zoo)
At Two.

Scraping a knee
At Three.

Ever asking for more
At Four.

Busy bee in a hive
At Five.

Playing war with sticks
At Six.

Running is heaven
At Seven.

I can't wait
To be Eight.

John Kitching

This is the hand

This is the hand
that touched the frost
that froze my tongue
and made it numb

this is the hand
that cracked the nut
that went in my mouth
and never came out

this is the hand
that slid round the bath
to find the soap
that wouldn't float

this is the hand
on the hot water bottle
meant to warm my bed
that got lost instead

this is the hand
that held the bottle
that let go of the soap
that cracked the nut
that touched the frost
this is the hand
that never gets lost.

Michael Rosen

8

Hands

Hands
handling
dangling in water
making and shaking
slapping and clapping
warming and warning
hitting and fitting
grabbing and rubbing
peeling and feeling
taking and breaking
helping and giving
lifting
sifting sand
hand holding
hand.

Peter Young

9

The Broken Toys

In the broken box
The broken toys—
    Dusty,
Battered and rusty,
Tattered and torn,
    Forlorn, forlorn.

The snapped strings
And the busted springs,
The rag-doll raggy and rent,
The pink tin teaset buckled and bent,
    The crashed plane,
    The car, the train—
Smashed in a terrible accident.

And all the dolls' eyes
Rolling loose like heavy marbles
Up the doll's house stairs and down
The stairs of the overturned house . . .
The dead wheels of a clockwork mouse .

In the broken box
The broken toys—
    Dusty,
Battered and rusty,
Tattered and torn,
    Forlorn, forlorn.

James Kirkup

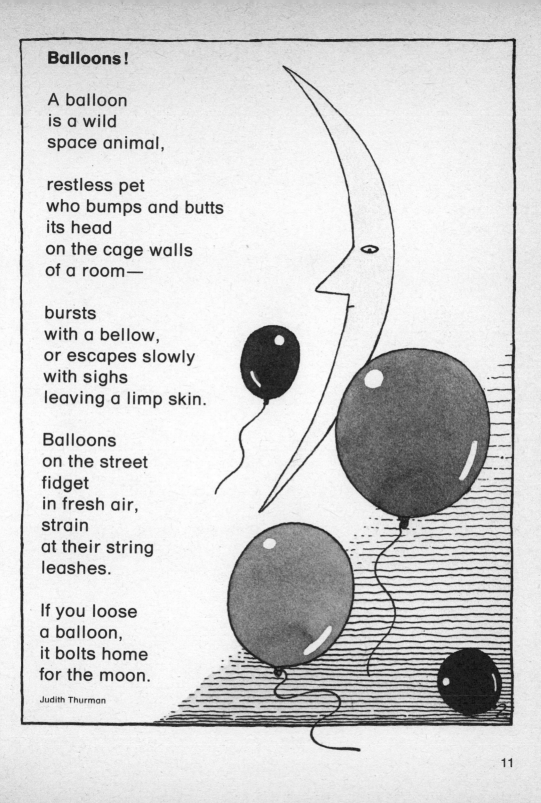

Balloons!

A balloon
is a wild
space animal,

restless pet
who bumps and butts
its head
on the cage walls
of a room—

bursts
with a bellow,
or escapes slowly
with sighs
leaving a limp skin.

Balloons
on the street
fidget
in fresh air,
strain
at their string
leashes.

If you loose
a balloon,
it bolts home
for the moon.

Judith Thurman

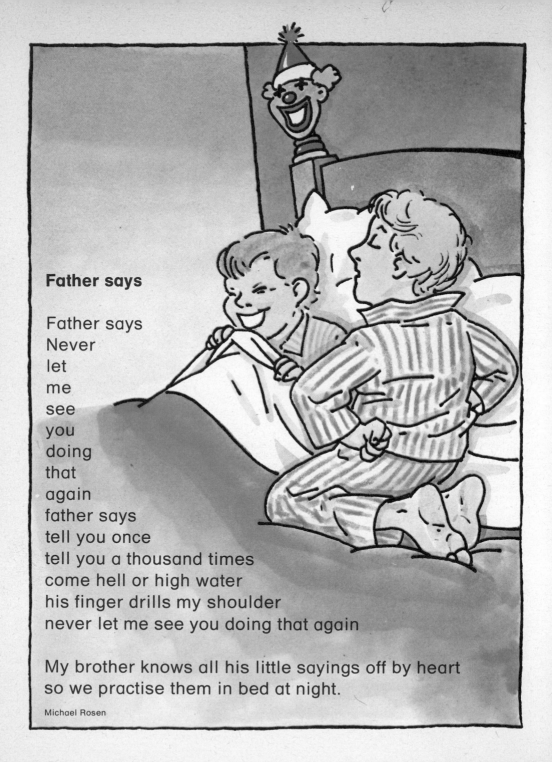

Father says

Father says
Never
let
me
see
you
doing
that
again
father says
tell you once
tell you a thousand times
come hell or high water
his finger drills my shoulder
never let me see you doing that again

My brother knows all his little sayings off by heart
so we practise them in bed at night.

Michael Rosen

What someone said when he was spanked on the day before his birthday

Some day
I may
Pack my bag and run away.
Some day
I may.
—But not today.

Some night
I might
Slip away in the moonlight.
I might.
Some night.
—But not tonight.

Some night.
Some day.
I might.
I may.
—But right now I think I'll stay.

John Ciardi

Hurry Home

You had better hurry home for your supper's nearly ready,
Your mother's in the kitchen and she's awfully wild,
She's been shouting at the cat, and she keeps on saying,
'O where has he got to, the wretched child?'

She has been to the front door and looked through the window
And now she's banging on the frying pan,
The plates and the dishes are all on the table,
So run, my boy, as fast as you can.

Don't you know she's cooking your favourite supper,
Potatoes in their jackets and beefsteak pie?
She's made a jug of custard for the pudding in the oven,
Get a move on, Joe, the stars are in the sky.

They've all left the factory, the streets will soon be empty,
No more playing now, it's time you fed,
It really is a shame to keep your mother waiting,
So come have your supper, and then off to bed.

Leonard Clark

Sad . . . and Glad

The sun has gone down,
Leaving an empty sky
   Above the hills
   Above our town.
Street-lamps switch on.
   Buses swish by.
Strangers are laughing.
My friends have gone in:
   I'm alone—
   It's time to go home.

Someone runs to the post,
   Leaving an open door—
   A family
   Makes itself toast
   Round the fire
   Down a long corridor.
   It's chilly,
And I've been out all day:
   I want my tea.
   It's time I was home.

They're calling in Tommy
   (I wish he was me);
   On the allotments
   Bonfire smoke rolls
   Sluggish, blue-grey.
   I'm still streets away:
   This time of year,
   This time of day,
     Makes me sad
   And glad—to get home.

Brian Lee

Flashlight

My flashlight tugs me
through the dark
like a hound
with a yellow eye,

sniffs
at the edges
of steep places,

paws
at moles'
and rabbits'
holes,

points its nose
where sharp things
lie asleep—

and then it bounds
ahead of me
on home ground.

Judith Thurman

16

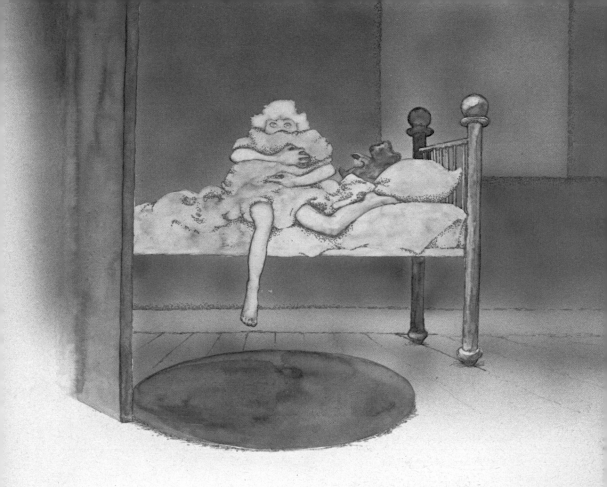

It's dark outside

It's dark outside.
It's dark inside.
It's dark behind the door.

I wonder
if I'm brave enough
to walk across the floor.

I am—
at least I think I am.
I'll try it once and see

if Mum comes up
or stays downstairs
with Dad and cups of tea.

Nancy Chambers

The sounds in the evening

The sounds in the evening
Go all through the house,
The click of the clock
And the pick of the mouse,
The footsteps of people
Upon the top floor,
The skirts of my mother
That brush by the door,
The crick in the boards,
And the creak of the chairs,
The fluttering murmurs
Outside on the stairs,
The ring of the bell,
The arrival of guests,
The laugh of my father
At one of his jests,
The clashing of dishes
As dinner goes in,
The babble of voices
That distance makes thin,
The mewings of cats
That seem just by my ear,
The hooting of owls
That can never seem near,

The queer little noises
That no one explains . . .
Till the moon through the slats
Of my window-blind rains,
And the world of my eyes
And my ears melts like steam
As I find in my pillow
The world of my dream.

Eleanor Farjeon

The Park

I'm glad that I
　　Live near a park
For in the winter
　　After dark
The park lights shine
　　As bright and still
As dandelions
　　On a hill.

James S. Tippett

In The Dark

A man runs across the ceiling
Of my bedroom,
Someone with long hands patterned with leaves.

The wardrobe looks like a huge bird,
Six times bigger than an eagle.
I don't like the dark.

The flowers on the table near the window
Catch the street light as it shines on them
Then they look like little heads.

When the wind blows it comes through the door,
And to me it sounds like a ghost
Worming its way through the cracks.
At night everything looks different
All sort of ghostly shapes
In the dark.

Jane Pridmore

The Bogus-Boo

The Bogus-boo
Is a creature who
Comes out at night—and why?
He likes the air;
He likes to scare
The nervous passer-by.

Out from the park
At dead of dark
He comes with huffling pad.
If, when alone,
You hear his moan
'Tis like to drive you mad.

He has two wings,
Pathetic things,
With which he cannot fly.
His tusks look fierce,
Yet could not pierce
The merest butterfly.

He has six ears,
But what he hears
Is very faint and small;
And with the claws
On his eight paws
He cannot scratch at all.

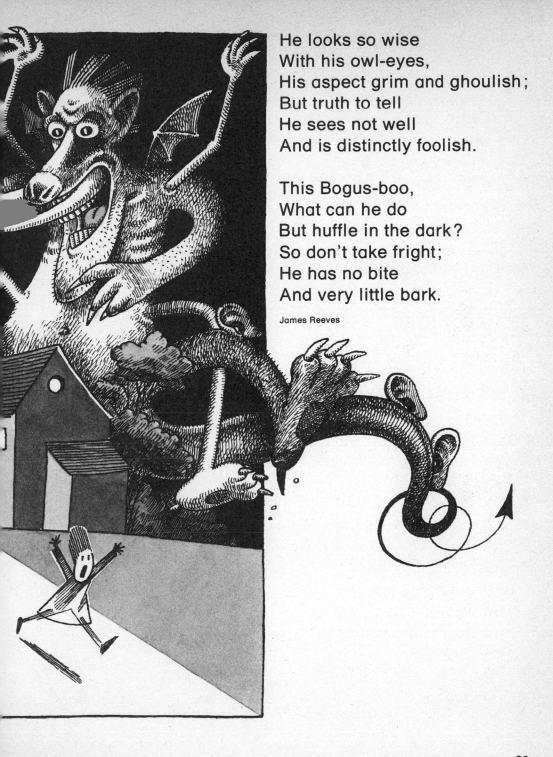

He looks so wise
With his owl-eyes,
His aspect grim and ghoulish;
But truth to tell
He sees not well
And is distinctly foolish.

This Bogus-boo,
What can he do
But huffle in the dark?
So don't take fright;
He has no bite
And very little bark.

James Reeves

I woke up this morning

I woke up this morning
at quarter past seven.
I kicked up the covers
and stuck out my toe.
And ever since then
(That's a quarter past seven)
They haven't said anything
Other than 'no'.

They haven't said anything
Other than 'Please, dear,
Don't do what you're doing,'
Or 'Lower your voice.'
And however I've chosen,
I've done the wrong thing
And I've made the wrong choice.

I didn't wash well
And I didn't say thank you.
I didn't shake hands
And I didn't say please.
I didn't say sorry
When, passing the candy,
I banged the box into
Miss Witelson's knees.
I didn't say sorry.
I didn't stand straighter.
I didn't speak louder
When asked what I'd said.

Well, I said
That tomorrow
At quarter past seven,
They can
Come in and get me
I'M STAYING IN BED.

Karla Kuskin

The Quarrel

I quarrelled with my brother,
I don't know what about,
One thing led to another
And somehow we fell out.
The start of it was slight,
The end of it was strong,
He said he was right,
I knew he was wrong!

We hated one another.
The afternoon turned black.
Then suddenly my brother
Thumped me on the back,
And said, 'Oh, *come* along!
We can't go on all night—
I was in the wrong.'
So he was in the right.

Eleanor Farjeon

She said I said he lied

She said I said he lied
but I said she said he lied
Then you said she said I said he lied.

He said he didn't lie.

Michael Rosen

I am the youngest in our house

I'm the youngest in our house
so it goes like this:

My brother comes in and says:
'Tell him to clear the fluff
out from under his bed.'
Mum says,
'Clear the fluff
out from under your bed.'
Father says,
'You heard what your mother
said.'
'What?' I say.
'The fluff,' he says.
'Clear the fluff
out from under your bed.'
So I say,
'There's fluff under his bed, too,
you know.'
So father says,
'But we're talking about the fluff
under *your* bed.'
'You will clear it up
won't you?' mum says.
So now my brother—all puffed up—
says,
'Clear the fluff
out from under your bed,
clear the fluff
out from under your bed.'

Now I'm angry. I am angry.
So I say—what shall I say?
I say,
'Shuttup stinks
YOU CAN'T RULE MY LIFE.'

Michael Rosen

My sister Laura

My sister Laura's bigger than me
And lifts me up quite easily.
I can't lift her, I've tried and tried;
She must have something heavy inside.

Spike Milligan

Going Through the Old Photos

Who's that?
That's your Auntie Mabel
and that's me
under the table.

Who's that?
That's Uncle Billy.
Who's that?
Me being silly.

Who's that
licking a lolly?
I'm not sure
but I think it's Polly.

Who's that
behind the tree?
I don't know,
I can't see.
Could be you.
Could be me.

Who's that?
Baby Joe.
Who's that?
I don't know.

Who's that standing
on his head?
Turn it round.
It's Uncle Ted.

Michael Rosen

30

When we go over to my grandad's

When we go over
to my grandads
he falls asleep.

While he's asleep
he snores.

When he wakes up,
he says,
'Did I snore?
did I snore?
did I snore?

Everybody says, 'No,
you didn't snore.'

Why do we lie to him?

Michael Rosen

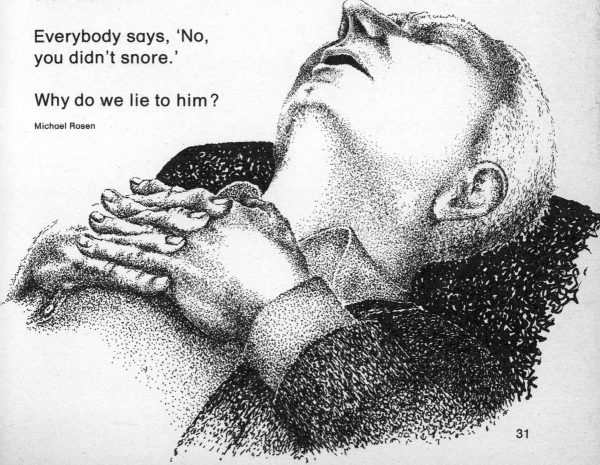

Zanzibar Pete and Zoom-along Dick

Zanzibar Pete and Zoom-along Dick
took a picnic to eat in the park.
They took so much food
(without being rude)
that they had to stay there until dark.

Zanzibar Pete and Zoom-along Dick
picked up all of the litter they'd made.
Then they felt so much thinner
they went home to dinner
and ate a lot more, I'm afraid.

Nancy Chambers

The Vulture

The Vulture eats between his meals,
    And that's the reason why
He very, very rarely feels
    As well as you and I.

His eye is dull, his head is bald,
    His neck is growing thinner.
Oh! what a lesson for us all
    To only eat at dinner.

Hilaire Belloc

Toffee-Slab

As thick as a plank, as unbending as Fate,
It was wrapped in wax-paper, and weighed like a slate;
It had a brown cow on it, smiling and fat
With 'rich' and 'creamy' and grand words like that:

And you broke it with bricks on Mrs Doig's wall,
So it came out irregular, but with something for all
(If you were quick, it was more or less fair—
Even Wee Andy had his proportional share);

Then with nobody speaking, with sort of fixed grins
And oozings like glue leaking over our chins
We'd stand there for ages, our eyes staring wide,
The great splinters of it jammed tightly inside,

With the sharpest end stuck, up near your brain,
What pleasure!—mingled with twinges of pain.

Brian Lee

Sweet Song

This is the sweet song,
Song of all the sweets,
Caramel and butterscotch
Bullseyes, raspberry treats;

Treacle toffee, acid drops,
Pastilles, crystal fruits,
Bubble-gum and liquorice-sticks
As black as new gum-boots;

Peppermint creams and aniseed balls,
Tiny sweets and whoppers,
Dolly-mixtures, chocolate drops,
Gigantic gob-stoppers;

Lemon sherberts, jelly babies,
Chocolate cream and flake,
Nougat, fudge and such as give
You tooth and belly-ache.

Vernon Scannell

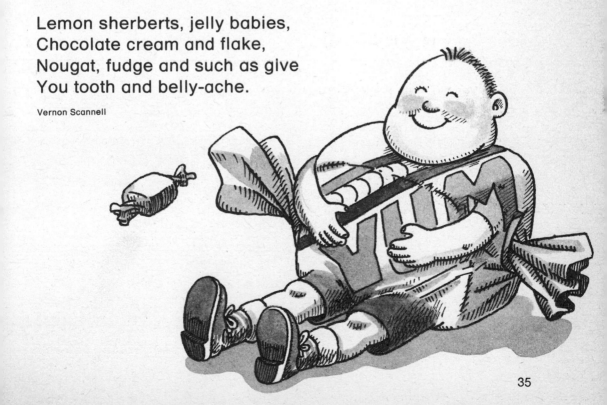

When Dad felt bad

One Sunday, Dad was feeling bad.
Pains in his head and tum, Mum said.

No dinner, Mum.
My head! My tum!

Dad said,
I bet
it's what I ate.

Too much to drink
said Mum,
I think.
Poor old chap,
Let him take a nap.

Then our cat, Ted,
jumped on the bed,
and put a mole
on poor Dad's head.

Dad jumped right up,
pyjamas down.
They heard him yell
all over town.

Quick! Quick!
said Dad.
Bring a big tin.

We put it down.
The mole ran in.

Down by the tree,
Dad set it free.

That's good, said Dad.
Now I feel fine.
I wonder if
it's dinner-time?

Charles Causley

The Dustbin Men

The older ones have gone to school,
My breakfast's on the plate,
But I can't leave the window-pane,
I might be just too late.

I've heard the clatter down the street,
I know they're creeping near,
The team of gruff-voiced, burly men
Who keep our dustbins clear.

And I must watch and see them clang
The dustbins on the road,
And stand in pairs to heave up high
The double-handled load.

Yes, there they come, the lorry growls
And grinds in bottom gear;
The dustman knees the garden gate
As, high up by his ear,
Firmly he balances the bin,
Head tilted to one side;
The great mouth of the rubbish cart
Is yawning very wide;
To me the mouth looks like a beast's,
A dragon's hungry jaws
That snap the refuse out of sight
Behind those sliding doors.

The lorry-dragon every day
Is in a ravenous mood,
And cardboard boxes, bottles, jars
Are all part of his food.

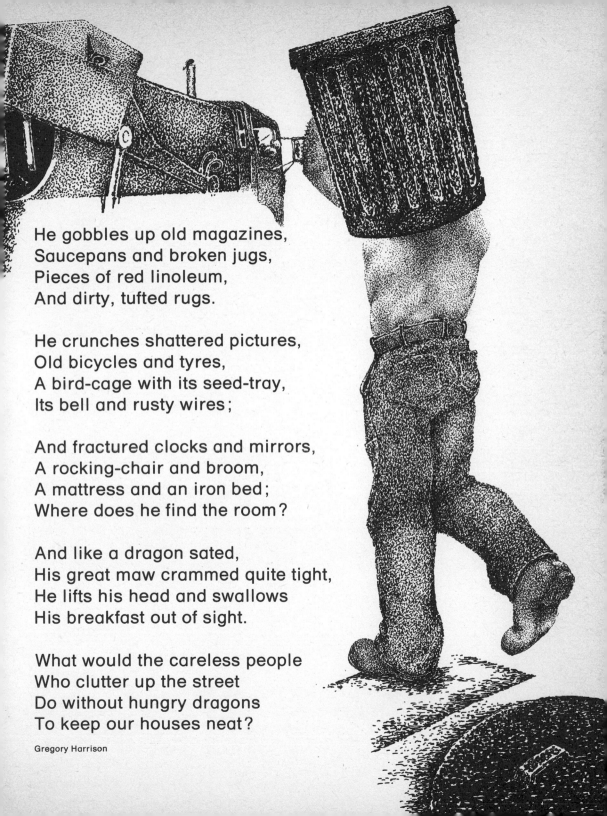

He gobbles up old magazines,
Saucepans and broken jugs,
Pieces of red linoleum,
And dirty, tufted rugs.

He crunches shattered pictures,
Old bicycles and tyres,
A bird-cage with its seed-tray,
Its bell and rusty wires;

And fractured clocks and mirrors,
A rocking-chair and broom,
A mattress and an iron bed;
Where does he find the room?

And like a dragon sated,
His great maw crammed quite tight,
He lifts his head and swallows
His breakfast out of sight.

What would the careless people
Who clutter up the street
Do without hungry dragons
To keep our houses neat?

Gregory Harrison

Mud

I like mud.
    I like it on my clothes.
I like it on my fingers.
    I like it in my toes.

Dirt's pretty ordinary
    And dust's a dud.
For a really good mess-up
    I like mud.

John Smith

Building Site

Men in
    Miles of mud;
    A sloshing
    Wash.

    Oceans of mud;
    A rain
    Drain.

Men like brown slugs on the
Drowned, brown, rain-washed plain.
    Straining cranes,
    Bucking trucks;
For men—too muddy much!

Pounds of caked mud
    Cling to each boot,
Mud ball-and-chain
In that brown rain drain—
    How can they lift a foot?

But in the end
Houses do get built on the silt.

Marian Lines

Motor Cars

From city window, 'way up high,
I like to watch the cars go by.
They look like burnished beetles, black,
That leave a little muddy track
Behind them as they slowly crawl.
Sometimes they do not move at all
But huddle close with hum and drone
As though they feared to be alone.
They grope their way through fog and night
With the golden feelers of their light.

Rowena Bastin Bennett

The Old Sussex Road

'Do I see a hat in the road?' I said.
I picked up the hat—and I saw a head.
I pulled out a man, who said, 'Don't go.
Help pull out my horse. He's down below.'

Ian Serraillier

Carbreakers

There's a graveyard in our street,
But it's not for putting people in;
The bodies that they bury here
Are made of steel and paint and tin.

The people come and leave their wrecks
For crunching in the giant jaws
Of a great hungry car-machine,
That lives on bonnets, wheels and doors.

When I pass by the yard at night,
I sometimes think I hear a sound
Of ghostly horns that moan and whine,
Upon that metal-graveyard mound.

Marian Lines

Let's send a rocket

Ten, nine, eight . . .
Seven, six, five . . .

We'll send up a rocket,
And it will be *live*.

Five, four, three . . .
It's ready to zoom!

We're counting each second,
And soon it will boom!

Get ready for . . . two;
Get ready to go . . .

It's *two*—and it's—*one*—
We're OFF! It's ZERO!

Kit Patrickson

44

The Aeroplane

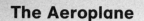

Aeroplane! Aeroplane!
Humming through the sky
Like a giant insect —
How I wish that I
   could fly too.

Seagull! Seagull!
White kite of the cliff-top,
Dipping and swooping —
How I wish that I
   had your wings.

Derek Stuart

45

The cliff-top

The cliff-top has a carpet
    Of lilac, gold and green:
The blue sky bounds the ocean
    The white clouds scud between.

A flock of gulls are wheeling
    And wailing round my seat;
Above my head the heaven,
    The sea beneath my feet.

Robert Bridges

The Ship

They have launched the little ship,
  She is riding by the quay.
Like a young doe to the river,
  She has trembled to the sea.

Her sails are shaken loose;
  They flutter in the wind.
The cat's-paws ripple round her
  And the gulls scream behind.

The rope is cast, she moves
  Daintily out and south,
Where the snarling ocean waits her
  With tiger-foaming mouth.

Richard Church

Going Barefoot

With shoes on,
I can only feel
how hard or soft
the rock or sand is
where I walk
or stand.

Barefoot,
I can feel
how warm mud
moulds my soles—
or how cold
pebbles
knead them
like worn knuckles.

Curling my toes,
I can drop
an anchor
to the sea floor—
hold fast
to the shore
when the tide
tows.

Judith Thurman

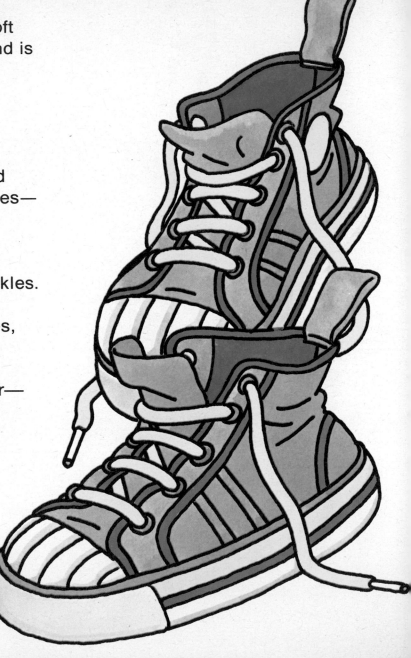

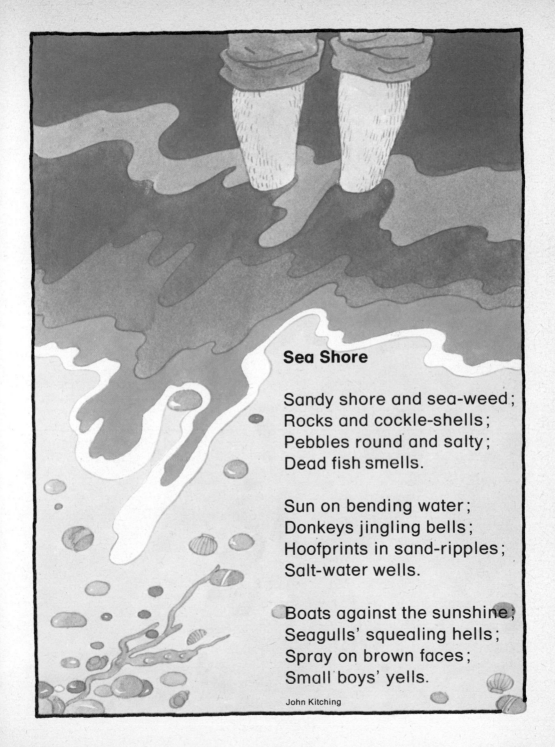

Sea Shore

Sandy shore and sea-weed;
Rocks and cockle-shells;
Pebbles round and salty;
Dead fish smells.

Sun on bending water;
Donkeys jingling bells;
Hoofprints in sand-ripples;
Salt-water wells.

Boats against the sunshine;
Seagulls' squealing hells;
Spray on brown faces;
Small boys' yells.

John Kitching

Seal

See how he dives
From rocks with a zoom!
See how he darts
Through his watery room
Past crabs and eels
And green seaweed,
Past fluffs of sandy
Minnow feed!
See how he swims
With a swerve and a twist,
A flip of the flipper,
A flick of the wrist!
Quicksilver-quick,
Softer than spray,
Down he plunges
And sweeps away;
Before you can think,
Before you can utter
Words like 'Dill pickle'
Or 'Apple butter',
Back up he swims
Past sting-ray and shark,
Out with a zoom,
A whoop, a bark;
Before you can say
Whatever you wish,
He plops at your side
With a mouthful of fish!

William Jay Smith

Flute Girl

Flute Girl, Flute Girl,
Sits by the sea.
Plays a sweet tune,
Plays a soft melody.

Flute Girl, Flute Girl,
Sits on the sand,
Sits, and her silver flute
Shines in her hand.

Flute Girl, Flute Girl,
Waits for the tide,
When her soft silver tune
Brings the seals to her side.

Flute Girl, Seal Girl,
See the seals play,
Close by the shore
At the end of the day.

Seal Girl, Seal Girl,
Plays her sweet tune,
As the seals' silver ripples
Shine in the moon.

Roderick Hunt

The Rescue

The wind is loud,
The wind is blowing,
The waves are big,
The waves are growing.
What's that? What's that?
A dog is crying,
It's in the sea,
A dog is crying.
His or hers
Or yours or mine?
A dog is crying,
A dog is crying.

Is no one there?
A boat is going,
The waves are big,
A man is rowing,
The waves are big,
The waves are growing.
Where's the dog?
It isn't crying.
His or hers
Or yours or mine?
Is it dying?
Is it dying?

The wind is loud,
The wind is blowing,
The waves are big,
The waves are growing.
Where's the boat?
It's upside down.
And where's the dog,
And must it drown?
His or hers
Or yours or mine?
O, must it drown?
O, must it drown?

Where's the man?
He's on the sand,
So tired and wet
He cannot stand.
And where's the dog?
It's in his hand,
He lays it down
Upon the sand.
His or hers
Or yours or mine?
The dog is mine,
The dog is mine!

So tired and wet
And still it lies.
I stroke its head,
It opens its eyes,
It wags its tail,
So tired and wet.
I call its name,
For it's my pet,
Not his or hers
Or yours, but mine—
And up it gets,
And up it gets!

Ian Serraillier

Bones

Bones is good with children,
He goes with us everywhere;
The beach, the park, the swimming-pool,
He comes to look us up at school—
He's stopped the Dodgems at the Fair.

Bones is good with children,
He does the same things as us;
Won't wipe his feet, won't shut the gate,
Goes off all day, then trails home late,
To *'Bad!'*, and bed, and fuss . . .

Bones is good with children,
He gets muddy and then he pongs
Of earth and burn and wood and pond,
The hills and all the moor beyond—
When it rains he rolls his eyes and longs

To be out with the children
And get himself soaked through,
Slide down the banks on tea-trays,
Chase sticks, and join our football-frays—
I think he'll even come with you:

'Cos Bones is good with children!

Brian Lee

Greedy Dog

This dog will eat anything.

Apple cores and bacon fat,
Milk you poured out for the cat.
He likes the string that ties the roast
And relishes hot buttered toast.
Hide your chocolates! He's a thief,
He'll even eat your handkerchief.
And if you don't like sudden shocks,
Carefully conceal your socks.
Leave some soup without a lid,
And you'll wish you never did.
When you think he must be full,
You find him gobbling bits of wool,
Orange peel or paper bags,
Dusters and old cleaning rags.

This dog will eat anything,
Except for mushrooms and cucumber.

Now what is wrong with those, I wonder?

James Hurley

Roger the Dog

Asleep he wheezes at his ease.
He only wakes to scratch his fleas.

He hogs the fire, he bakes his head
As if it were a loaf of bread.

He's just a sack of snoring dog.
You can lug him like a log.

You can roll him with your foot,
He'll stay snoring where he's put.

I take him out for exercise,
He rolls in cowclap up to his eyes.

He will not race, he will not romp,
He saves his strength for gobble and chomp.

He'll work as hard as you could wish
Emptying his dinner dish,

Then flops flat, and digs down deep,
Like a miner, into sleep.

Ted Hughes

Cats

Cats sleep
Anywhere,
Any table,
Any chair,
Top of piano,
Window-ledge,
In the middle,
On the edge,
Open drawer,
Empty shoe,
Anybody's
Lap will do,
Fitted in a
Cardboard box,
In the cupboard
With your frocks—
Anywhere!
They don't care!
Cats sleep
Anywhere.

Eleanor Farjeon

58

Cat

My cat has got no name,
We simply call him Cat;
He doesn't seem to blame
Anyone for that.

For he is not like us
Who often, I'm afraid,
Kick up quite a fuss
If *our* names are mislaid.

As if, without a name,
We'd be no longer there
But like a tiny flame
Vanish in bright air.

My pet, he doesn't care
About such things as that:
Black buzz and golden stare
Require no name but Cat.

Vernon Scannell

Yellow Cat

'There he is,' yells Father,
Grabbing lumps of soil,
'That yellow tabby's on the fence.
Drown him in boiling oil.
He's scratching at my runner beans.
Bang at the window, quick.
Wait till I get my laces done
I'll beat him with my stick.'

'Too late,' they shout, 'he's on the fence.
He's turning, Father, wait.'

'I'll give him turning, I'll be there,
I'll serve him on a plate.'

They banged the window, Father stormed
And hopped with wild despair;
The cat grew fat with insolence
And froze into a stare.
Its brazen glare stopped Father
With its blazing yellow light;
The silken shape turned slowly
And dropped gently out of sight.

Gregory Harrison

61

Grumblers

Why, O why,
did you make me cry?
The angry words you said
keep echoing in my head,
and all because I did not feed
my budgie with his breakfast seed.

For all your alarm,
he has come to no harm,
has been happy all day
singing my tears away;
does not look sad or thin
though I put no water in his tin,
or gave him fresh sand,
so, why can't you understand
we all make mistakes?
And, O, how my heart aches
that I neglected my bird;
but don't say another word,
just go through the door,
leave me alone,
to grieve on my own;
I don't want you to see
my misery.

He's there in the kitchen now
like any bird on bough,
the whole house he fills
with his wonderful trills;
glad to be home with us,
he does not grumble or fuss.

Leonard Clark

Mare

When the mare shows you
her yellow teeth, stuck
with clover and gnawed leaf,
you know they have combed
pastures of spiky grasses,
and tough thickets.

But when you offer her
a sweet, white lump
from the trembling plate
of your palm—she trots
to the gate, sniffs—
and takes it with velvet lips.

Judith Thurman

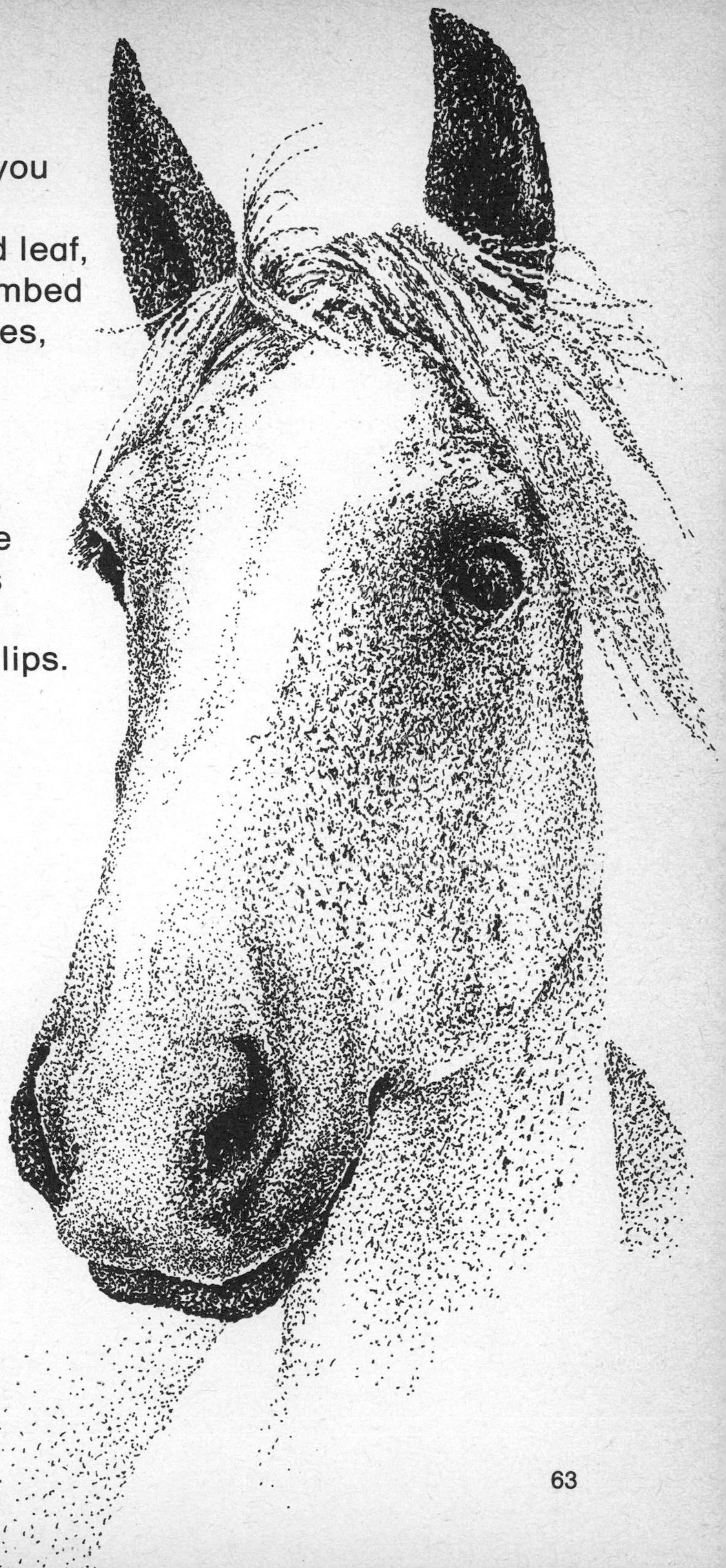

63

The small brown bear

The small brown bear
fishes
with stony paws

eating ice salmon
all waterfall slippery
till his teeth ache.

Michael Baldwin

64

Arctic Vixen

The snowfox
the winter fox

is the colour
of bushy snow

her breath
like a white brush

and her eye
rusty.

Michael Baldwin

Gabble-Gabble

'Gabble-gabble! gabble-gabble!'
The seven fat geese say.
'Gabble-gabble! gabble-gabble!'
In the green field all day.

'Gabble-gabble'—never stopping,
While the sun sweeps the sky.
Gabble-gabble go the seven geese,
And I will tell you why.

Those seven geese sat in the hot sun
In the meadow long ago,
And through the hedge came the red fox
And spied them all in a row.

'Ho ho!' said he with a wicked grin
And a glint in his hungry eye.
'I never saw such a dinner before,
And today those geese must die!'

'Oh no, Sir Fox, have pity on us!'
They cry with anguish shrill.
'Sir Fox,' they plead, 'it is not right
Such poor weak birds to kill.'

'Fat, foolish geese, your wailing cease,'
Said the red fox in his greed.
'Fat, foolish geese, prepare to die;
Your plaints I will not heed.'

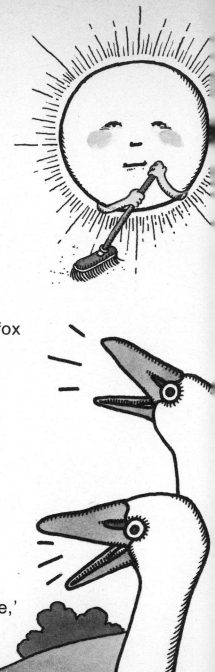

'Oh then, Sir Fox,' the first goose said,
'If our lives you will not spare,
Take us and eat us, one and all,
But first let us say a prayer.

'Gladly we give ourselves to you
When we have prayed to heaven,
For we shall be the sweeter fare
If our sins be forgiven.'

'A pious thought,' the fox agreed.
'Pray on, pray on, I say!
I will not touch you, foolish geese,
Till you have ceased to pray.'

So 'gabble-gabble' the seven geese prayed
From sunrise to sunset.
'Gabble-gabble' to heaven they cry
And have not left off yet.

James Reeves

Porwigles

Six porwigles
Wriggling in a pool,
Pretending to be whales
And trying to keep cool.
One porwigle whale
Tried a flying dive—
When they had a tail count
There were only five.

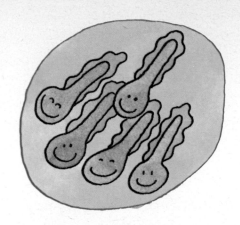

Five porwigles
Wriggling in a pool,
Pretending to be whales
And trying to keep cool.
One porwigle whale
Went off to explore—
When they had a tail count
There were only four.

Four porwigles
Wriggling in a pool,
Pretending to be whales
And trying to keep cool.
One porwigle whale
Went to find the sea—
When they had a tail count
There were only three.

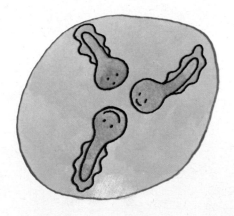

Three porwigles
Wriggling in a pool,
Pretending to be whales
And trying to keep cool.
One porwigle whale
Didn't like the view—
When they had a tail count
There were only two.

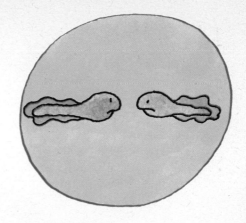

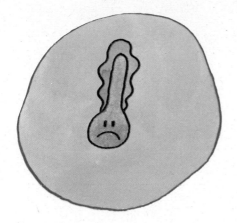

Two porwigles
Wriggling in a pool,
Pretending to be whales
And trying to keep cool.
One porwigle whale
Went to see his Mum—
Left the last one on his own,
There is only one.

One porwigle
Wriggling in a pool,
Feeling rather lonely
And trying to keep cool.
One all alone porwigle
Jumped onto a log—
And you couldn't count *his* tail
Because he's turned into a frog!

Julie Holder
Porwigle is an old English name for a tadpole.

The Frog's Lament

'I can't bite
like a dog,'
said the bright
green frog.

'I can't nip,
I can't squirt,
I can't grip,
I can't hurt.

'All I can do
is hop and hide
when enemies come
from far and wide.

'I can't scratch
like a cat.
I'm no match
for a rat.

'I can't stab,
I can't snare,
I can't grab,
I can't scare.

'All I can do
my whole life through
is hop,' said the frog,
'and hide from view.'

And that's
what I saw him
up and do.

Aileen Fisher

A centipede

A centipede can run at great speed,
Because of his number of legs,
But when he hangs out his socks to dry,
It costs him a fortune in pegs.

A centipede likes to wear wellington boots,
But because of his centipede brain,
It takes such a time to sort out all the pairs
That he's never in time for the rain.

A centipede has one hundred legs,
But I'm glad that I haven't because
When the front of a centipede gets where it's going
His back end is still where it was.

Julie Holder

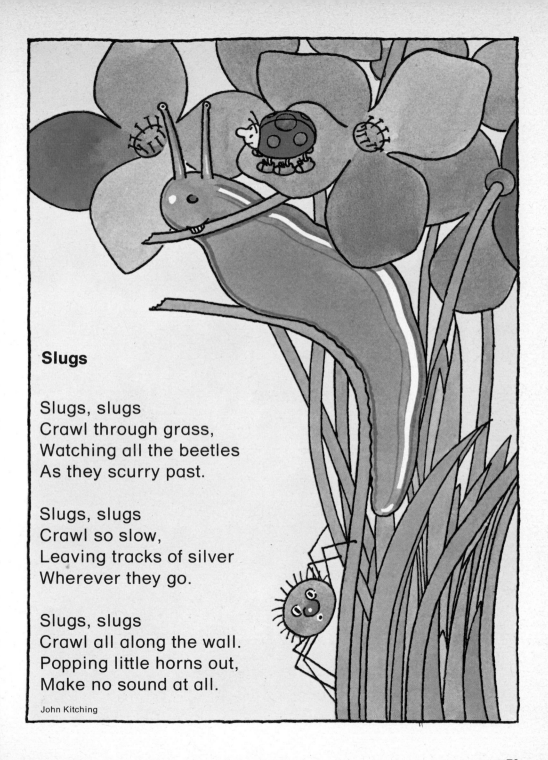

Slugs

Slugs, slugs
Crawl through grass,
Watching all the beetles
As they scurry past.

Slugs, slugs
Crawl so slow,
Leaving tracks of silver
Wherever they go.

Slugs, slugs
Crawl all along the wall.
Popping little horns out,
Make no sound at all.

John Kitching

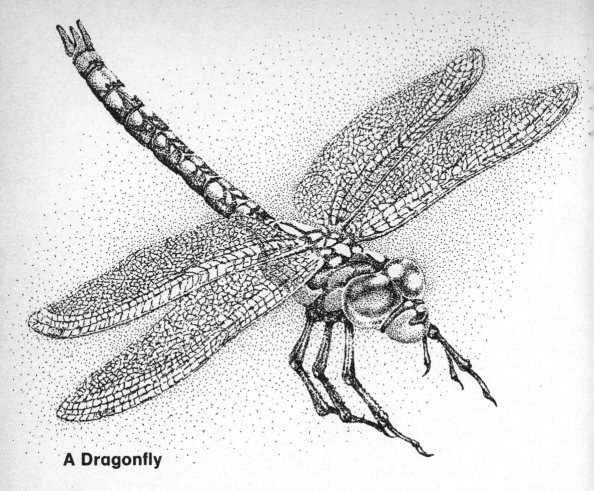

A Dragonfly

When the heat of the summer
Made drowsy the land,
A dragonfly came
And sat on my hand.

With its blue-jointed body,
And wings like spun glass,
It lit on my fingers
As though they were grass.

Eleanor Farjeon

August afternoon

Where shall we go?
    What shall we play?
What shall we do
    On a hot summer day?

We'll sit in the swing.
    Go low. Go high.
And drink lemonade
    Till the glass is dry.

One straw for you,
    One straw for me,
In the cool green shade
    Of the walnut tree.

Marion Edey

There's a red brick wall

There's a red brick wall
    along our street
that stands and burns
    in the sun's hot heat.

There aren't any flames
    but I know it burns.
When I walk by,
    it glows and turns
    my face to fire.

Nancy Chambers

Swimming in the town

The swimming pool is closed—
There isn't any money.
What shall we do?
It isn't very funny.

We'll open up the school
And chase away the porter,
Turn on the taps
And fill it up with water.

Ian Serraillier

The Pines

Hear the rumble,
Oh, hear the crash.
The great trees tumble.
The strong boughs smash.

Men with saws
Are cutting the pines—
That marched like soldiers
In straight green lines.

Seventy years
Have made them tall.
It takes ten minutes
To make them fall.

And breaking free
With never a care,
The pine cones leap
Through the clear, bright air.

Margaret Mahy

Holes of green

Trees are full of holes—
between the leaves I mean.
But if you stand away enough
the holes fill up with green.

Aileen Fisher

What is Red?

Red is a sunset
Blazing and bright.
Red is feeling brave
With all your might.
Red is a sunburn
Spot on your nose.
Sometimes red
Is a red red rose.
Red squiggles out
When you cut your hand.
Red is a brick
And the sound of a band.
Red is hotness
You get inside
When you're embarrassed
And want to hide.
Fire-cracker, fire-engine
Fire-flicker red—

And when you're angry
Red runs through your head.
Red is an Indian,
A Valentine heart,
The trimmings on
A circus cart.
Red is a lipstick
Red is a shout
Red is a signal
That says: 'Watch out!'
Red is a great big
Rubber ball.
Red is the giant-est
Colour of all.
Red is a show-off,
No doubt about it—
But can you imagine
Living without it?

Mary O'Neill

The Kite

How bright on the blue
Is a kite when it's new!

With a dive and a dip
It snaps its tail

Then soars like a ship
With only a sail

As over tides
Of wind it rides,

Climbs to the crest
Of a gust and pulls,

Then seems to rest
As wind falls.

When string goes slack
You wind it back

And run until
A new breeze blows

And its wings fill
And up it goes!

How bright on the blue
Is a kite when it's new!

But a raggeder thing
You never will see

When it flaps on a string
In the top of a tree.

Harry Behn

The Wind

I can get through a doorway without any key,
And strip the leaves from the great oak tree.

I can drive storm clouds and shake tall towers,
Or steal through a garden and not wake the flowers.

Seas I can move and ships I can sink;
I can carry a house-top or the scent of a pink.

When I am angry I can rave and riot;
And when I am spent, I lie quiet as quiet.

James Reeves

84

Clouds

Wonder where they come from?
Wonder where they go?
Wonder why they're sometimes high
and sometimes hanging low?
Wonder what they're made of,
and if they weigh a lot?
Wonder if the sky feels bare
up there
     when clouds are *not*?

Aileen Fisher

Windy Nights

Whenever the moon and the stars are set,
    Whenever the wind is high,
All night long in the dark and wet,
    A man goes riding by.
Late in the night when the fires are out,
Why does he gallop and gallop about?

Whenever the trees are crying aloud,
    And ships are tossed at sea,
By, on the highway, low and loud,
    By at the gallop goes he.
By at the gallop he goes, and then
By he comes back at the gallop again.

Robert Louis Stevenson

Flying

I saw the moon
One windy night,
Flying so fast—
All silvery white—
Over the sky,
Like a toy balloon
Loose from its string—
A runaway moon.
The frosty stars
Went racing past,
Chasing her on
Ever so fast.
Then everyone said,
'It's the clouds that fly,
And the stars and moon
Stand still in the sky.'
But I don't mind—
I saw the moon
Sailing away
Like a toy
Balloon.

J. M. Westrup

The night will never stay

The night will never stay,
The night will still go by,
Though with a million stars
You pin it to the sky;
Though you bind it with the blowing wind
And buckle it with the moon,
The night will slip away
Like sorrow or a tune.

Eleanor Farjeon

Winter Morning

Winter is the king of showmen,
Turning tree stumps into snow men
And houses into birthday cakes
And spreading sugar over lakes.
Smooth and clean and frosty white,
The world looks good enough to bite.
That's the season to be young,
Catching snow flakes on your tongue.

Snow is snowy when it's snowing,
I'm sorry it's slushy when it's going.

Ogden Nash

Death of a snowman

I was awake all night,
Big as a polar bear,
Strong and firm and white.
The tall black hat I wear
Was draped with ermine fur.
I felt so fit and well
Till the world began to stir.
And the morning sun swell.
I was tired, began to yawn;
At noon in the humming sun
I caught a severe warm;
My nose began to run.
My hat grew black and fell,
Was followed by my grey head.
There was no funeral bell,
But by tea-time I was dead.

Vernon Scannell

There was an old man

There was an old man
Had a face made of cake,
He stuck it with currants
And put it in to bake.

The oven was hot,
He baked it too much,
It came out covered
With a crunchy crust.

The eyes went pop,
The currants went bang,
And that was the end
Of that old man.

James Kirkup

Giant Jojo

I am Jojo
give me the sun to eat.
I am Jojo
give me the moon to suck.

The waters of my mouth
will put out the fires of the sun;
the waters of my mouth
will melt the light of the moon.

Day becomes night,
night becomes day.
I am Jojo
listen to what I say.

Michael Rosen

Alone in the Grange

Strange,
Strange,
Is the little old man
Who lives in the Grange.
Old,
Old;
And they say that he keeps
A box full of gold.
Bowed,
Bowed,
Is his thin little back
That once was so proud.
Soft,
Soft,

Are his steps as he climbs
The stairs to the loft.
Black,
Black,
Is the old shuttered house.
Does he sleep on a sack?

They say he does magic,
That he can cast spells,
That he prowls round the garden
Listening for bells;
That he watches for strangers,
Hates every soul,
And peers with his dark eye
Through the keyhole.

I wonder, I wonder,
As I lie in my bed,
Whether he sleeps with his hat on his head?
Is he really magician
With altar of stone,
Or a lonely old gentleman
Left on his own?

Gregory Harrison

Uncle James

My uncle James
Was a terrible man.
He cooked his wife
In the frying pan.

'She's far too tender
To bake or boil!'
He cooked her up
In peanut oil.

But sometime later—
A month or more—
There came a knock
On my uncle's door.

A great green devil
Was standing there.
He caught my uncle
By the hair.

'Are you the uncle
That cooked his wife,
And leads such a terribly
Wicked life?'

My uncle yowled
Like an old tom cat,
But the devil took him
For all of that.

Oh, take a tip
From my Uncle James!
Don't throw stones
And don't call names.

Just be as good
As ever you can—
And never cook aunts
In a frying pan!

Margaret Mahy

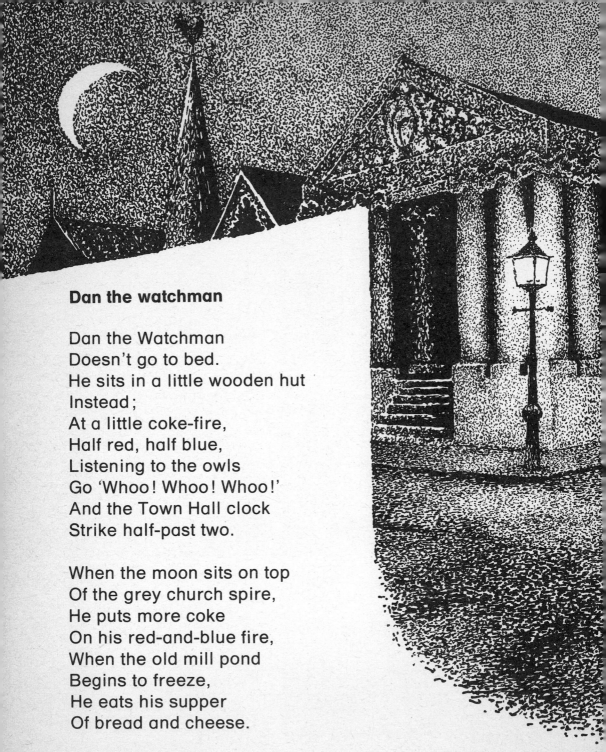

Dan the watchman

Dan the Watchman
Doesn't go to bed.
He sits in a little wooden hut
Instead;
At a little coke-fire,
Half red, half blue,
Listening to the owls
Go 'Whoo! Whoo! Whoo!'
And the Town Hall clock
Strike half-past two.

When the moon sits on top
Of the grey church spire,
He puts more coke
On his red-and-blue fire,
When the old mill pond
Begins to freeze,
He eats his supper
Of bread and cheese.

I'd like to go out
In the middle of the night,
When the little coke fire
Is shining bright,
When the flames turn blue,
And the flames burn red,
And everyone else in the world is in bed.
Then I'd sit in the little wooden hut with Dan
And drink strong tea from his black billy can.

John D. Sheridan

Herbaceous Plodd

Herbaceous Plodd
is rather odd.
His eyes are red,
his nose is blue,
his neck and head
are joined by glue.
He only dines
on unripe peas,
bacon rinds
and melted cheese.
He rarely talks,
he never smiles,
but goes for walks
with crocodiles.

Michael Dugan

100

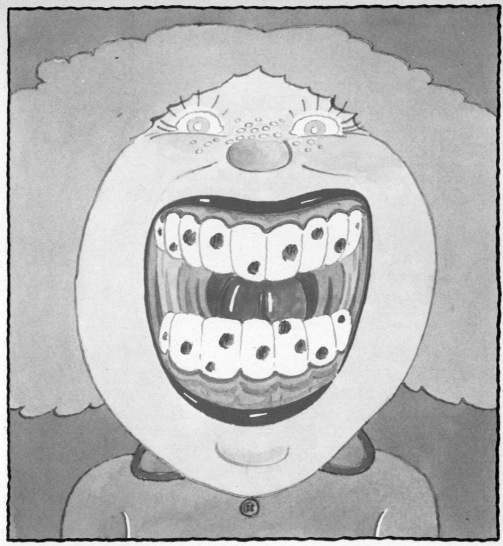

Rosemary's teeth

Rosemary Freeth
had holes in her teeth,
deeper than ten metre rules.
So she said with a shout—
'Take all my teeth out
and I'll sell them for swimming pools.'

Michael Dugan

Scarecrow Independence

I may look raggy and queer
—but I bow to no man.

My face may look silly and sad
—but I'm no snowman.

I may stand stiff and still
—but hold my head high.

I raise my old top hat to no one
—not even when *you* walk by.

James Kirkup

Ella McStumping

Ella McStumping
was fond of jumping.
From tables and chairs,
bookshelves and stairs
she would jump to the floor
then climb back for more.
At the age of three
she climbed a high tree
and with one mighty cry
she leapt for the sky.
Doctor McSpetter
says she'll get better,
and the hospital say
she can come home next May,
and Ella McStumping
has given up jumping.

Michael Dugan

Thin Jake

My old friend Jake
was as thin as a snake
and light as a drop of rain.
One windy day
Jake blew away
and was never seen again.

Michael Dugan

The radio men

When I was little more than six
I thought that men must be
Alive inside the radio
To act in plays, or simply blow
Trumpets, or sing to me.

I never got a glimpse of them,
They were so very small.
But I imagined them in there,
Their voices bursting on the air
Through that thin, wooden wall.

Elizabeth Jennings

The Little Wee Man

As I was walking all alone
Between a river and a wall,
There I saw a little wee man—
I'd never seen a man so small.

His legs were barely a finger long,
His shoulders wide as fingers three;
Light and springing was his step,
And he stood lower than my knee.

He lifted a stone six feet high,
He lifted it up to his right knee,
Above his chest, above his head,
And flung it as far as I could see.

'O,' said I, 'how strong you are!
I wonder where your home can be.'
'Down the green valley there;
O will you come with me and see?'

So on we ran, and away we rode,
Until we came to his bonny home;
The roof was made of beaten gold,
The floor was made of crystal stone.

Pipers were playing, ladies dancing,
Four-and-twenty ladies gay;
And as they danced they were singing,
'Our little wee man's been long away.'

Out went the lights, on came the mist.
Where were the ladies? Where was he?
I looked and saw the wall and river . . .
That was all that I could see.

Ian Serraillier

The Marrog

My desk's at the back of the class
    And nobody, nobody knows
        I'm a Marrog from Mars
With a body of brass
    And seventeen fingers and toes.

Wouldn't they shriek if they knew
    I've three eyes at the back of my head
        And my hair is bright purple
My nose is deep blue
    And my teeth are half-yellow, half-red.

My five arms are silver, and spiked
    With knives on them sharper than spears.
I could go back right now if I liked—
    And return in a million light-years.

I could gobble them all
For I'm seven foot tall
    And I'm breathing green flames from my ears.

Wouldn't they yell if they knew,
    If they guessed that a Marrog was here?
Ha-ha, they haven't a clue—
        Or wouldn't they tremble with fear!
'Look, look, a Marrog'
    They'd all scream—and **SMACK**
The blackboard would fall and the ceiling would crack
    And teacher would faint, I suppose.
But I grin to myself, sitting right at the back
    And nobody, nobody knows.

R. C. Scriven

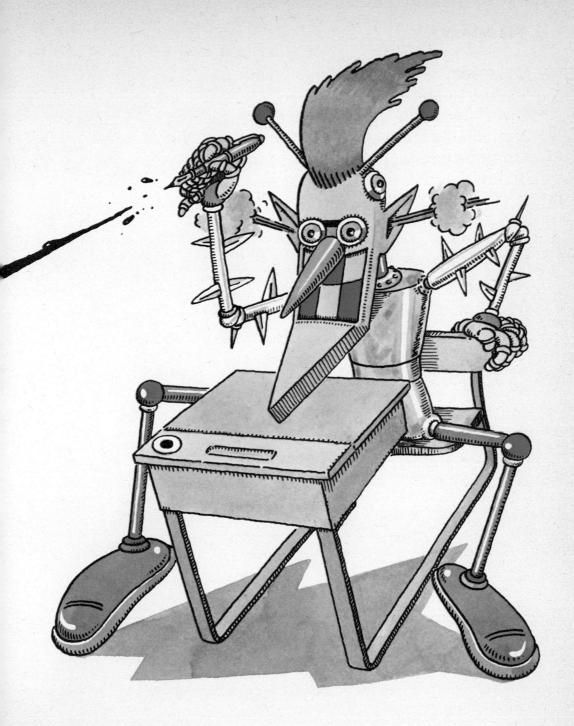

Mixed Brews

There once was a witch
Who lived in a ditch
And brewed her brews in the hedges.
She gathered some dank
From the deepest bank
And some from around the edges.

She practised her charms
By waving her arms
And muttering words and curses;
And every spell
Would have worked out well
If she hadn't mixed the verses.

Not long since
When she wanted a Prince
To wake the Sleeping Beauty,
A man appeared
With a long grey beard
Too old to report for duty.

When she hoped to save
Aladdin's cave
From his uncle cruel and cranky,
She concocted a spell
That somehow fell
Not on him but on Widow Twankey.

With a magic bean
She called for a Queen
Who was locked in the wizard's castle.
There came an old hag
With a postman's bag
And threepence to pay on the parcel.

What *comes* of a witch
Who has hitch after hitch?
I'm afraid that there's no telling:
But I think, as a rule,
She returns to school
And tries to improve her spelling.

Clive Sansom

House

The ruins of an old house stand
Without a roof, on muddy land,
Each window is a sightless eye
Staring at the city sky.

Locks are broken, every wall
Looks as if about to fall.
The people who lived here, they say,
Just packed up and went away.

And once when I was playing there
Halfway up the curving stair
I thought I heard a laughing sound
Coming from the trampled ground.

Leonard Clark

The Man Who Wasn't There

Yesterday upon the stair
I met a man who wasn't there;
He wasn't there again today,
I wish, I wish, he'd go away.

I've seen his shapeless shadow-coat
Beneath the stairway, hanging about;
And outside, muffled in a cloak
The same colour as the dark;

I've seen him in a black, black suit
Shaking, under the broken light;
I've seen him swim across the floor
And disappear beneath the door;

And once, I almost heard his breath
Behind me, running up the path;
Inside he leant against the wall,
And turned . . . and was no one at all.

Yesterday upon the stair
I met the man who wasn't there;
He wasn't there again today,
I wish, I wish, he'd go away.

Brian Lee

The Silent Spinney

What's that rustling behind me?
Only a cat.
Thank goodness for that,
For I'm afraid of the darkness,
And these tall trees
Are silent and black,
And if ever I get out of here, mate,
I can tell you I'm not coming back.

There's a dark shadow out in the roadway,
See if there's someone behind that tree,
For I'm afraid of the darkness
And it might jump out at me.

My sisters are scared stiff of spiders,
My mother is frightened of mice,
But I'm afraid of the darkness,
I'm not coming this way twice.

Seamus Redmond

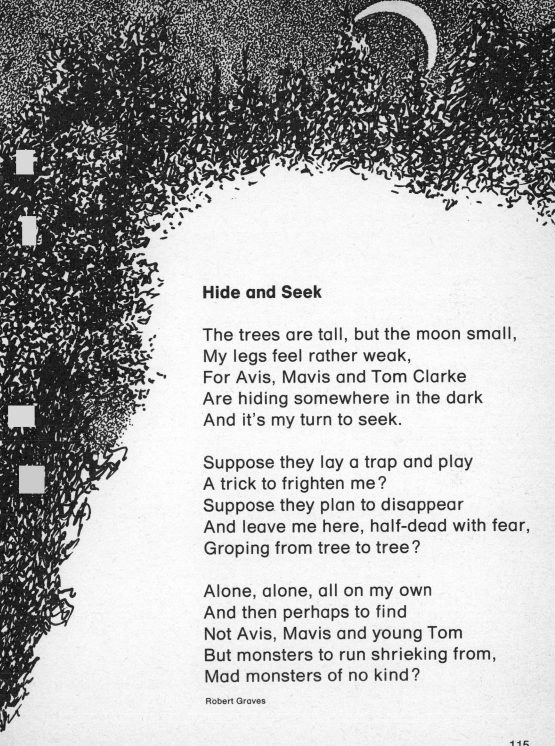

Hide and Seek

The trees are tall, but the moon small,
My legs feel rather weak,
For Avis, Mavis and Tom Clarke
Are hiding somewhere in the dark
And it's my turn to seek.

Suppose they lay a trap and play
A trick to frighten me?
Suppose they plan to disappear
And leave me here, half-dead with fear,
Groping from tree to tree?

Alone, alone, all on my own
And then perhaps to find
Not Avis, Mavis and young Tom
But monsters to run shrieking from,
Mad monsters of no kind?

Robert Graves

Cold Feet

They have all gone across
They are all turning to see
They are all shouting 'come on'
They are all waiting for me.

I look through the gaps in the footway
And my heart shrivels with fear,
For far below the river is flowing
So quick and so cold and so clear.

And all that there is between it
And me falling down there is this:
A few wooden planks—not very thick—
And between each, a little abyss.

The holes get right under my sandals.
I can see straight through to the rocks,
And if I don't look, I can feel it,
Just there, through my shoes and my socks.

Suppose my feet and my legs withered up
And slipped through the slats like a rug?
Suppose I suddenly went very thin
Like the baby that slid down the plug?

I know that it cannot happen
But suppose that it did, what then?
Would they be able to find me
And take me back home again?

They have all gone across
They are all waiting to see
They are all shouting 'come on'—
But they'll have to carry me.

Brian Lee

Lonely boy

Lonely boy, lonely boy
Let me play with you
I'm on my own
I'm all alone
And you've nobody too.

John Kitching

What?

What's in the room I have never entered,
In the heavy gloom when the velvet is drawn?
What's under the bed, or inside the wardrobe,
    In my own room when I wake up at dawn?

No one knows what's in there in the cupboard
    When everyone else has gone out,
In the silence that follows the slam of the door,
    After dark, when no one's about;
At the back of the brooms and old shirts and old socks,
The hoover, the shoes, those queer things in a box,
    In the thick smell of polish
In the darkest cobwebby corner where the roof slopes down to
    the floor.

What's behind the door I have never opened?
    What is at the end of the corridor?
What's round the next bend in the empty lane,
    Further than I have ever been before?

Brian Lee

118

Closet

I like to
pretend

the raincoat
sleeves
are the leaves.

I like to
pretend

the slippery
boots
are the roots.

I like to
pretend

the old fur coat
is my friend,
the brown bear,

who lets me
hide
in her lair.

Judith Thurman

Secrets

Some questions they won't answer.
   I ask, 'Why not?' They say
'Because you would not understand.
   You will some day.'

But there are things I've noticed
   That I can't talk about—
The shapes of hands, or faces;
   A fear; a doubt.

'A penny for your thoughts, 'they say;
   But though they're old and grand,
I cannot talk—because they would
   Not understand!

Edward Lowbury

120

The Spinning Earth

The earth, they say,
spins round and round.
It doesn't look it
from the ground,
and never makes
a spinning sound.

And water never
swirls and swishes
from oceans full
of dizzy fishes,
and shelves don't lose
their pans and dishes.

And houses don't go whirling by,
or puppies swirl around the sky,
or robins spin instead of fly.

It may be true
what people say
about one spinning
night and day . . .
but I keep wondering, anyway.

Aileen Fisher

I wonder

I wonder why the grass is green,
And why the wind is never seen.

Who taught the birds to build a nest,
And told the trees to take a rest?

O, when the moon is not quite round,
Where can the missing bit be found?

Who lights the stars, when they blow out,
And makes the lightning flash about?

Who paints the rainbow in the sky,
And hangs the fluffy clouds so high?

Why is it now, do you suppose,
That Dad won't tell me, if he knows?

Jeannie Kirby

Who?

Who made the sky?
Who made the earth?
Who thought of my or anyone's birth?

Who made the stars?
Who made the moon?
Who thought of night or morning or noon?

Who made the bees?
Who made the grass?
Who made the bonnie wee laddie and lass?

Who made the sun?
Who made the rain?
Who thought of the horse's tail and mane?

Who made the trees?
Who made them tall?
Won't somebody tell me who made it all?

Jane Catermull

Index of first lines

A balloon 11
A centipede can run at great speed 72
A man runs across the ceiling 21
Aeroplane! Aeroplane! 45
As I was walking all alone. 106
As thick as a plank, as unbending as Fate. 34
Asleep he wheezes at his ease 56
Bones is good with children 54
Cats sleep 58
Dan the Watchman 98
'Do I see a hat in the road?' I said 42
Ella McStumping. 103
Father says 12
Flute Girl, Flute Girl 51
From city window, way up high 42
'Gabble-gabble! gabble-gabble!' 66
Hands 9
Hear the rumble 78
Herbaceous Plodd 100
How bright on the blue. 82
I am Jojo. 93
I can get through a doorway without any key 84
I can't bite 70
I like mud 40
I like to 119
I may look ragged and queer 102
I quarrelled with my brother 26
I saw the moon 87
I was awake all night 91
I woke up this morning. 24
I wonder why the grass is green 122
I'm glad that I. 20
I'm the youngest in our house 28

In the broken box 10
It's dark outside 17
Lonely boy, lonely boy 117
Men in 41
My cat has got no name 59
My desk's at the back of the class 108
My flashlight tugs me 16
My old friend Jake 104
My sister Laura's bigger than me 29
My Uncle James 96
Not having much fun 7
One Sunday, Dad was feeling bad 36
Red is a sunset 80
Rosemary Freeth 101
Sandy shore and sea-weed 49
See how he dives 50
She said I said he lied 27
Six porwigles 68
Slugs, slugs 73
Some day 13
Some questions they won't answer 120
Strange 94
Ten, nine, eight 44
The Bogus-Boo 22
The cliff-top has a carpet 46
The earth, they say 121
The night will never stay 88
The older ones have gone to school 38
The ruins of an old house stand 112
The small brown bear 64
The snow fox 65
The sounds in the evening 18
The sun has gone down 15

The swimming pool is closed 77
The trees are tall, but the moon small 115
The Vulture eats between his meals 33
The wind is loud 52
'There he is,' yells Father 60
There once was a witch 110
There was an old man 92
There's a graveyard in our street 43
There's a red brick wall 76
They have all gone across 116
They have launched the little ship 47
This dog will eat anything 55
This is the hand 8
This is the sweet song 35
Trees are full of holes 79
What's in the room I have never entered? 118
What's that rustling behind me? 114
When I was little more than six 105
When the heat of the summer 74
When the mare shows you 63
When we go over 31
Whenever the moon and the stars are set 86
Where shall we go? 75
Who made the sky? 123
Who's that? 30
Why, oh why 62
Winter is the king of showmen 98
With shoes on 48
Wonder where they come from? 85
Yesterday upon the stair 113
You had better hurry home, for your supper's nearly ready   14
Zanzibar Pete and Zoom-along Dick 32

Acknowledgements

The Editor and Publisher wish to thank the following for permission to reprint copyright poems in this anthology. Although every effort has been made to contact the owners of the copyright in poems published here, a few have been impossible to trace, but if they contact the Publisher, correct acknowledgement will be made in future editions.

Harry Behn: From *Windy Morning*, Copyright 1953 by Harry Behn, reprinted by permission of Harcourt Brace Jovanovich. Hilaire Belloc: From *Cautionary Verse*, published 1941 by Alfred A. Knopf, Inc., and reprinted by permission of Gerald Duckworth & Co. Ltd., and Alfred A. Knopf, inc. Rowena Bennett: From *Songs Around a Toadstool Table*, Copyright © 1967 by Rowena Bennett, reprinted by permission of Follett Publishing Company, a division of Follett Corporation. Robert Bridges: From *The Poetical Works of Robert Bridges*, reprinted by permission of Oxford University Press. Jane Catermull: From *Elizabethan Poetry Awards Competition*, reprinted by permission of World's Work Ltd. Charles Causley: From Macmillan Little Nippers *When Dad Felt Bad* (Macmillan), reprinted by permission of David Higham Associates Ltd. Nancy Chambers: From *Stickleback, Stickleback* (Kestrel Books, 1977), Copyright © Nancy Chambers, 1977, reprinted by permission of Penguin Books Ltd. Richard Church: From *Collected Poems* (William Heinemann Ltd.), reprinted by permission of Laurence Pollinger Ltd., on behalf of the Estate of the late Richard Church. John Ciardi: From *You Know Who*, Copyright © 1964 by John Ciardi, reprinted by permission of J. B. Lipincott Company. Leonard Clark: 'Hurry Home' from *Here and There*, reprinted by permission of Shufunotomo Co. Ltd. 'House' from *Collected Poems and Verses for Children*, reprinted by permission of Dennis Dobson Publishers. Michael Dugan: From *My Old Man* (Trend Series, 1976), reprinted by permission of Longman Cheshire Pty. Ltd. Marion Edey: From *Open the Door* by Marion Edey and Dorothy Grider, Copyright 1949 Marion Edey and Dorothy Grider, reprinted with the permission of Charles Scribner's Sons. Eleanor Farjeon: From *Silver Sand and Snow* (Michael Joseph), reprinted by permission of David Higham Associates Ltd. Aileen Fisher: 'The Frog's Lament', 'Holes of Green' and 'Clouds' from *In the Woods, In the Meadow, In the Sky* (World's Work Ltd. and Charles Scribner's Sons) reprinted by permission of World's Work Ltd. and the author. 'The Spinning Earth' from *I Wonder How, I Wonder Why* (Abelard–Schumann), reprinted by permission of the author. Robert Graves: From *The Poor Boy Who Followed His Star and Children's Poems* (Cassells), reprinted by permission of A. P. Watt Ltd., on behalf of Robert Graves. Gregory Harrison: From *The Night of the Wild Horses*, © Gregory Harrison 1971, reprinted by permission of the author and Oxford University Press. Julie Holder: From *The Flumps Annual*, 1978 (World Distributors Ltd.), reprinted by permission of the author. James Hurley: From *If You Should Meet a Crocodile*, ed. Margaret Mayo, (Kaye & Ward), reprinted by permission of the author. Jeannie Kirby: From *Come Follow Me*, reprinted by permission of Evans Brothers Ltd. James Kirkup: 'The Broken Toys' and 'There Was an Old Man' from *Round About Nine* (Frederick Warne), reprinted by permission of Dr. Jan Van Loewen Ltd. on behalf of the author. John Kitching: 'Sea Shore' and 'Slugs' from *Hi-Ran-Ho!*, eds. Aiden and Nancy Chambers (Longman Young Books, 1971), Copyright © John Kitching, 1971, reprinted by permission of Penguin Books Ltd. Karla Kuskin: From *The Rose on My Cake*, Copyright © 1964 by Karla Kuskin, reprinted by permission of Harper & Row, Publishers, Inc. Elizabeth Jennings: From *The Secret Brother*, reprinted by permission of Macmillan, London and Basingstoke. Brian Lee: 'The Man Who Wasn't There', 'Cold Feet', and 'What?', from *Late Home* (Kestrel Books, 1976), Copyright © 1976 by Brian Lee, reprinted by permission of Penguin Books Ltd. Marion Lines: From *Tower Blocks*, reprinted by permission of Franklin Watts Ltd. Edward Lowbury: From *Green Magic* (Chatto & Windus), reprinted by permission of the author. Margaret Mahy: From *The First Margaret Mahy Story Book*, reprinted by permission of J. M. Dent & Sons Ltd. Spike Milligan: From *Silly Verse for Kids*, reprinted by permission of Dennis Dobson Publishers. Ogden Nash: From *Parents Keep Out* (J. M. Dent & Sons), reprinted by permission of A. P. Watt Ltd. on behalf of The Estate of the late Ogden Nash. Also from *The Nutcracker Suite and Other Innocent Verses*, Copyright © 1961, 1962 by Ogden Nash, reprinted by permission of Little, Brown & Company. Mary O'Neill: From *Hailstones and Halibut Bones*, Copyright © 1961 by Mary Le Duc O'Neill, reprinted by permission of World's Work Ltd., and Doubleday & Company, Inc. Kit Patrickson: From *Poems for Me*, reprinted by permission of Ginn & Company Ltd. Seamus Redmond: From *BBC Poetry Corner* – Autumn 1968, reprinted by permission of the author. James Reeves: 'The Bogus Boo' from *More Prefabulous Animiles*, and 'The Wind' from *The Wandering Moon*, reprinted by permission of Wm. Heinemann Ltd. Michael Rosen: 'I'm the Youngest in our House' from *Wouldn't You Like to Know*, reprinted by permission of Andre Deutsch Ltd. 'This is the Hand' and 'Father Says' from *Mind Your Own Business!*, Copyright © 1974 by Michael Rosen, reprinted by permission of Andre Deutsch Ltd., and S. G. Phillips, Inc. Clive Sansom: From *The Golden Unicorn* (Methuen), reprinted by permission of David Higham Associates. Vernon Scannell: 'Cat' and 'Death of a Snowman' from *The Apple-Raid and Other Poems*, reprinted by permission of Chatto & Windus Ltd. R. C. Scriven: From *Journeys*, Spring 1968 (BBC Publications), reprinted by permission of the author. Ian Serraillier: 'The Rescue', 'No Swimming in the Town' and 'The Little Wee Man' from *I'll Tell You a Tale* (Puffin Books), Copyright © 1976 by Ian Serraillier and Puffin Books, reprinted by permission of the author. John D. Sheridan: From *Stirabout Lane*, reprinted by permission of J. M. Dent & Sons Ltd. John Smith: From *The Early Bird and The Worm* (Burke Books), reprinted by permission of the author. William Jay Smith: From *Boy Blue's Book of Beasts* (Atlantic Monthly Press, Little Brown Co.), Copyright © 1957 by William Jay Smith, reprinted by permission of Curtis Brown Ltd., New York. Judith Thurman: From *Flashlight and Other Poems* (Kestrel Books, 1977) Copyright © 1976 by Judith Thurman, reprinted by permission of Penguin Books Ltd., and Atheneum Publishers. James Tippett: From *Crickety Cricket! The Best Loved Poems of James S. Tippett*, text Copyright © 1973 by Martha K. Tippett, reprinted by permission of World's Work Ltd., and Harper and Row, Publishers, Inc. James Westrup: From *Come Follow Me*, reprinted by permission of Evans Brothers Ltd. Peter Young: From *Passwords One*, reprinted by permission of Oliver and Boyd.

The following poems are being published for the first time in this anthology and appear by permission of their author, unless otherwise indicated.
Michael Baldwin: 'The Small Brown Bear' and 'Arctic Vixen' both Copyright © 1979 by Michael Baldwin. Leonard Clark: 'Grumblers', Copyright © 1979 by Leonard Clark. Ted Hughes: 'Roger the Dog', Copyright © 1979 by Ted Hughes. Roderick Hunt: 'Flute Girl', Copyright © 1979 by Roderick Hunt. James Kirkup: 'Scarecrow Independence', Copyright © 1979 by James Kirkup. John Kitching: 'Can't Wait', and 'Lonely Boy' both Copyright © 1979 by John Kitching. Brian Lee: 'Sad . . . and Glad', 'Toffee Slab' and 'Bones' all Copyright © 1979 by Brian Lee. James Reeves: 'Gabble, Gabble', Copyright © 1979 by James Reeves Estate; published by permission of the James Reeves Estate. Michael Rosen: 'She Said I Said He Lied', 'Going Through Old Photos', 'When We Go Over to my Grandad's' and 'Giant Jojo', all Copyright © 1979 by Michael Rosen. Vernon Scannell: 'Sweet Song', Copyright © 1979 by Vernon Scannell. Ian Serraillier: 'The Old Sussex Road', Copyright © 1979 by Ian Serraillier. Derek Stuart: 'Aeroplane! Aeroplane!', Copyright © 1979 by Derek Stuart.

Printed by Chorley & Pickersgill Ltd Leeds
Phototypeset by Tradespools Ltd., Graphic House, South Parade, Frome, Somerset